**Und**
**Day**
**ii**

C000083083

# Understand
# Day Trading
# in a Day

## Second Edition

**Ian Bruce**

GLOBAL
professional
*publishing*

Apart from any fair dealing for the purpose of research or private study, or criticism or review, as permitted under the Copyright, Designs and Patents Act 1988, this publication may only be reproduced, stored or transmitted, in any form or by any means, with the prior permission in writing of the publisher, or in the case of reprographic reproduction in accordance with the terms and licences issued by the Copyright Licensing Agency. Enquiries concerning reproduction outside those terms should be addressed to the publisher. The address is below.

Global Professional Publishing Limited Ltd
Random Acres
Slip Mill Lane
Hawkhurst
Cranbrook
Kent TN18 5AD
http: www.gppbooks.com

© Global Professional Publishing Ltd 2009
New Edition 2009

The moral right of the author has been asserted.

All rights reserved. No part of this book may be reproduced in any form or by any means without permission in writing from the publisher, except by a reviewer who may quote brief passages in a review.

ISBN: 978-1-906403-13-3

Printed by Replika Press, India

**You should take independent financial advice before acting on material contained in this book.**

For full details of Global Professional Publishing titles in Finance, Banking and Management see our website at:
www.gppbooks.com

# Contents

## Acknowledgements

I would like to dedicate this newly revised third edition of
*Understand Bonds & Gilts In A Day* to my wife Pauline and to
my children Hannah and Zachary.

Thanks to Alex Kiam for allowing me to reproduce some of his
excellent technical analysis work in chapters six through nine.

My thanks to Chris Brown for his support in writing the original
edition of this book, and to Global Professional Publishing for
publishing this new edition.

## About the Author

Ian Bruce is a successful businessman and the author of more
than a dozen books on finance, entrepreneurship and personal
development, all of which enjoy a wide international audience.
Best known for his ability to present complex ideas in a simple
and down to earth manner, he currently resides in mid Wales.

# Introduction

*Day trading is the new rock and roll of the investment world. Learn to day trade and you could quit your nine to five job and make a fortune from the comfort of your own home. If the market goes up, you can make big money. If the market goes down, you can still make big money. All you need to know is how! So start studying day trading today! Some people have become millionaires by day-trading, and so could you!*

That's the hype of day-trading which is often used to sell training courses, study manuals, computer software programmes and seminars. But this kind of hype only tells half the story, so before you rush to hand in your letter of resignation, let me sober you up a little with a few facts from the dark half of the coin...

♦ Day trading is not all sunshine and roses. Whilst some people have indeed made vast fortunes from home by day trading successfully, many more have lost money. Indeed, according to one survey in the USA, some seventy per cent of people who day trade go on to lose money.

♦ The ability to day trade successfully is not something that you can master in a week or a fortnight, no matter how expensive the seminar you attend or the study materials you purchase (though, of course, you **can** understand it in a day)! Learning to day trade successfully takes a lot of time, effort and, yes, money.

◆ It is true that day trading can be done by anyone with sufficient funds. But this doesn't mean that day trading is suitable for all types of investors. On the contrary, day trading is a highly specialised way of investing which suits only a small proportion of investors.

The aim of *Understand Day Trading In A Day* is not to encourage you to become a day trader, nor is it intended to discourage you. The aim is simply to provide you with a balanced and unbiased introduction to the phenomenon of day trading. It is written with the assumption that you want facts, not hype, and that once you have a sound basic knowledge of the subject you are intelligent enough to decide for yourself whether or not day trading is for you.

We will begin our study in Chapter 1 by looking at exactly what day trading is and what it involves. We will also discuss how a day trader differs from the more traditional type of investor. Then, in Chapter 2, we will discuss how the markets work and what factors make them move up, down or sideways.

In the following three chapters we'll examine what a day trader needs to have the greatest chance of succeeding. Not only will we discuss the technology of day trading, but also the knowledge required and the mindset of day trading success.

Chapters 6 through 9 take a detailed look at some of the actual day trading strategies used to predict and profit from market movements. In these chapters you will learn about moving averages, stochastics and other technical indicators.

Finally, having covered all of these subjects, we conclude by taking a look at the future of day trading and ask if day trading is just a passing craze as some people believe, or whether is really is something that is here to stay.

On a side issue: in many places through this book, for ease, I use the masculine gender when referring to day traders - writing "he or she" in every instance would be very clumsy. This gender use should not be taken as a reflection on who makes a successful day trader, especially as some of the most successful traders I know are female.

Once again, let me reiterate the fact that I personally have no vested interested in taking any particular view of day trading. My aim in this concise guide is simply to provide you with a balanced and honest introduction to the subject so that you can then make your own decision whether day trading is or isn't something you would like to get involved in.

On that basis, welcome to **Understanding Day Trading In A Day**.

**Ian Bruce**
July, 2009

**Chapter One**

# What is
# Day Trading?

---

**Key Concept:**
Day trading is exactly what the term suggests -
the opening and closing of any trading position on the
same day. Any individual who trades in this way
is referred to as a day trader.

---

The definition of day trading is simple enough to grasp. A day trade is a trading position that is both opened and closed on the same day. The amount of time between the opening and closing of a position can be seconds, minutes or hours. One thing remains constant however, and that is the fact that a day trader never leaves any position open overnight.

*Jon buys 1,000 shares in a company for £5 each. Two hours later the price of the shares have risen to £5.10. He sells all 1,000 shares to realise a profit of £100.*

This is a simple day trade. The trading position is opened when Jon buys his 1,000 shares. Two hours later the position is closed when he sells them. On this occasion the trade has generated a profit. Sometimes a trade generates a loss. However, the aim of the day trader is not necessarily to win every time he trades. His aim is to trade as often as possible within any given day, and to win more often than he loses, so that a profit is generated at the end of each day, however small that profit may be.

Of course, just because a day trader aims to make a daily profit doesn't mean he will always succeed. Even the most experienced day trader sometimes arrives at the end of the day showing a loss. In these cases the trader must simply accept the loss as an unfortunate fact of life, and then focus their mind on that fact that tomorrow they will have plenty of opportunities to recoup what they have lost - and possibly more besides.

Even at this early stage you should already be concluding that day trading deviates quite a lot from conventional investing wisdom. That wisdom tells us to "buy and hold" our investments for the long haul, riding out market volatility in the fairly certain hope of making a good percentage profit in three, four or five years time. Day traders, in comparison, forget the long haul. They aim to get in, get out and make a profit all in the same day. And, preferably, to do so several times a day!

This is by no means the only difference between the day trader and the more traditional investor. Here are some of the other major differences to note:

## Traders Trade, Investors Invest

It's an obvious point, but one which is commonly overlooked. The day trader is primarily a trader. He isn't usually too interested in what he buys or sells, only that he makes a profit on the trade as a whole. The traditional investor, on the other hand, is very interested in where his money goes, since this money may well be tied up in any given company for several years at a time.

## Traders Don't Mind Volatility

Volatility, the sharp and sudden movements of a market going up and down, is what gives the day trader the opportunity to generate profits several times each day. A successful trader can open a financial position, wait for the position to rise in value and then close it for a profit. He can then wait for the market to dip down again before repeating the whole process in order to aim for yet another bite at the same cherry.

The traditional investor doesn't usually like volatility. Instead they view it as a miserable fact of life that markets can go down as well as up, and would much rather prefer them to move more smoothly so they feel more secure.

## Traders Aren't Passive

Traditional investors generally like to be fairly passive when it comes to making money. Of course, many of them like to hand-pick their own shares and keep a close eye on their portfolios, but apart from those duties they prefer to leave their money alone to grow steadily over several months or years.

The day trader is a far more aggressive individual as far as his money is concerned. He watches the markets like a hawk and is quick to take advantage of any profitable trading opportunity he finds. For a trader, the idea of only making money by passively investing over the long haul is about as unappealing as an idea can get - not because he doesn't value long-term investing strategies, but because he likes to take the bull by the horns and create wealth in a more active manner.

## Traders Swing Both Ways

The traditional investor generally makes his profits as the stock-market makes gains. He buys shares and holds on to them for several weeks, months or years in the belief that by the time he comes to sell, the shares he has purchased will be worth more than when he purchased them.

The day trader, by comparison, can make money whether the market goes up or down. In fact, some of the biggest day trading fortunes have been made by individuals who correctly predicted dramatic stock market corrections - even crashes - which left most traditional investors out in the cold.

You will discover how it is possible for a day trader to profit from downwards trends as well as upward trends later on in this chapter.

# Is the Day Trader an Investor or a Gambler?

This is a question which many people ask when they first begin to take a closer look at the subject of day trading - and the short answer is that a day trader can be either. It all depends on the psychological make up of the individual involved.

A person who operates as a real-time, hands-on investor will open and close positions according to factual information and technical analysis indicators (see Chapters 6-9). Of course, in doing so he is taking a risk, but that risk is an informed one. He knows when to cut his losses if a market moves against him and he does so every time. He works in a highly disciplined, almost machine-like manner, being careful to adhere to a strict set of personal rules which he knows are vital for long term success as a day trader.

A person who has the mindset of a gambler, on the other hand, will tend to open and close financial positions according to gut feelings. He will expose himself to variable risks according to his moods and attitudes at the time. He knows when to cut his losses if a market moves against him, but often decides to "hang in for while longer" in the hope that the market will turn around in his favour. As for personal rules, his creed is to fly by the seat of his pants. Long-term success seldom enters his mind. What this gambler wants is profit right now, come hell or high water.

Obviously, individuals who have the mindset of a gambler seldom do well in the world of day trading. Sure, some of them get lucky and make short-term profits, just as some people at a roulette wheel hit a couple of lucky winning numbers. But, long-term, the gambler will always tend to lose more money than he wins.

Day trading itself then, is a neutral activity. For some people it presents an opportunity to gamble according to hunches, luck and mood swings. For others it presents a very real opportunity to profit from legitimate investment knowledge, skill and discipline. What day trading means to you is a decision only you can make.

# Which Financial Instruments Can Be Day-Traded?

Although most people think of trading company shares when they think of day trading, equities are really just the tip of the iceberg. There are several other financial instruments that can be day-traded effectively. Let us now look at the most popular financial instruments used by day-traders on a regular basis...

## Company Shares

Just as a traditional investor can buy shares in companies such as British Petroleum, British Telecom, Dell, IBM and so on, so the day trader can day trade these company shares. Of course, when a day trader is looking to day trade in shares, he isn't looking for long term profitability. He is most probably looking for shares which are quite volatile and regularly experience short-term price swings which he can potentially profit from in a matter of minutes or hours.

A day trader can profit from company shares in one of two ways.

The first way of generating profit is by taking the route of the traditional investor. The trader buys x number of shares, waits for the price to rise and then sells them in order to realise a profit.

The second way a day trader can generate profits from shares is by "selling short". This is a facility offered by some brokers which allows the trader to borrow shares from the broker and then sell them in the hope of buying back at a lower price later that day. When this is achieved the 'shares' are then paid back to the broker. Selling short has long been very popular, but financial regulators in many countries have been willing to temporarily outlaw short selling in times of particular economic difficulty, so it is important to be aware that this can happen.

# Share Options

Share options are financial products in their own right, which can be used to generate profits from share price fluctuations without buying the shares themselves. To put it very simply, they give the day trader the right - but not the obligation - to buy or sell shares at a predetermined price. There are two types of share options, and these are:

◆ **Call Options** which give the trader the right to **buy** shares at a known price.

◆ **Put Options** which give the trader the right to **sell** shares at a known price.

Share options are bought in units of one contract, and a contract gives the trader control over a certain number of shares (usually 1,000) for a limited period. The price which will be paid for the shares is known as the exercise price and the date on which the contract expires is known as the expiry date.

This option to buy or sell shares is obviously valuable in its own right, and the buyer will have to pay a premium, which is commonly referred to as the option price or price of the options Option prices move according to the type of contract and the movement of the underlying share price. If the underlying share price goes down then a call option (which gives the right to buy shares) will also go down, but a put option (which gives the right to sell shares) will go up.

On the other hand, if the underlying share price goes up then a call option will also go up, but a put option will go down.

As far as the day trader is concerned, trading in options gives him a tremendous amount of leverage, since an option is almost always cheaper than the shares themselves. This allows the trader to gain control over many more shares by buying options than he could by using the same amount of money to buy the underlying shares.

Because of this, the underlying share price doesn't have to move nearly so far in order for the day trader to succeed in making a profit.

For more detailed information on options, please see *Investing in Traded Options* by Robert Linggard, also published by TTL.

# Index Options

Just as a share option allows the day trader to make money by correctly predicting whether a share price will go up or down, so index options allow the day trader to do the same with market indices such as the FTSE 100, NASDAQ and so on.

A market index is a figure which reflects the state of the shares within that particular index. The FTSE 100, for example, reflects the state of the top one hundred FTSE shares. If the majority of shares in the FTSE 100 increase in value then the FTSE 100 index will rise. If the majority of shares in the FTSE 100 decrease in value then the FTSE 100 index will fall.

By buying index options (calls or puts, as with share options) the day trader can generate profits by correctly predicting whether any given market index will rise or fall. The more a market moves in the direction he had predicted, the more profits he can expect to make before he closes his position.

## Commodity Futures

Commodity Futures are similar to options in that they enable the day trader to purchase a contract representing a fixed amount of oil, pork bellies, gold, corn, wheat and so on. The price of the future in question rises or falls according to the value of the underlying commodity.

Only the most professional day traders tend to trade commodity futures. This is because being able to predict movements in commodity values requires a very detailed knowledge not only of market indicators, but also of several external factors such as how the weather will affect corn crops, and so on.

# The Pros and Cons of Day Trading

There are both positive and negative factors to think about when considering day trading, and the main ones can be identified as follows:

# The Advantages of Day Trading

## Wealth

Yes, day trading can make you wealthy. If a day trader knows his stuff, is able to predict market movements accurately and, equally importantly, is able to open and close positions at the right time, then he can make more money in a day than most other people earn in a month - sometimes much more.

Exactly how much wealth can a day trader gain? The answer to this question depends on several factors such as how much money the trader risks in each trade, how often he closes a position profitably and how often he trades. Obviously, the richest traders are those who risk sizeable sums many times each day and close the majority of their positions to realise a profit.

## Convenience

Day trading is a convenient occupation for many people. Most day traders work from the comfort of their own homes, either in a spare bedroom or in a purpose-built office. They work when they want and as often as they want. Some traders are happy to make a living by completing just one or two trades each day, and to take the rest of the day off to play golf or spend more time with their families. Other traders enjoy the trading experience so much that they will quite happily spend twelve hours each day opening and closing many positions.

However, in either case, the way in which the day trader fits work into their life is up to them. Day trading can therefore allow the trader to enjoy a level of convenience which most people only ever dream of.

## Independence

Closely tied in with the advantage of convenience is that of independence. Day traders are generally private individuals who work for themselves with their own money and equipment. They have no boss, supervisor or other individual to answer to. They make their own decisions in their own way, and are fully resp-onsible for their own success or failure as a day trader.

To some, such a high level of independence may be viewed as a bad thing. But for an increasing number of people, it is a dream come true.

# The Disadvantages of Day Trading

## Success isn't easy

Successful day trading isn't easy. You can't just buy a book, study it over a weekend and make it happen on the next Monday morning. To become successful as a day trader you need to spend hours, weeks and months learning all you can about the subject as fully as you are able.

In addition, success requires the development of commitment, patience, optimism, self-discipline and a host of other personal qualities which most people, it has to be said, don't have in great amounts. And of course, on top of all that, the aspiring day trader needs money to start trading with.

# Losses

All day traders suffer losses, especially in the early months of their activities. Theoretical knowledge gained through the study of books, attending seminars and so on can all help increase a day trader's chances of success, but inevitably there are lessons which can only be learned the hard way: from making mistakes which cost money - sometimes a great deal of money.

# Equipment

Whilst the more traditional investor can make good profits by buying and selling shares over the telephone with nothing more than the information on television and in the newspaper to help them make their investment decisions, the day trader needs much more. He needs access to the latest stock market prices, a constant awareness of breaking news stories that might be relevant and, last but not least, a computer set-up which enables him to open and close positions at the touch of a button.

Of course, if day trading really is for you then these disadvantages aren't likely to be disadvantages at all - they are just part of the day-trading life. And let's make no bones about it, day trading really is a way of life. Those who succeed don't treat it as a hobby or a fun way to kill a few hours. Instead they live, breath and sleep day trading - even when they're out of their office playing golf. If that idea doesn't put you off, then maybe day trading is something you could benefit from.

# Summary

◆ Day Trading is exactly what the term suggests: the opening and closing of any trading position on the same day.

◆ Any individual who trades in this way is referred to as a day trader.

◆ Day traders differ from traditional investors in a number of ways. They aim to make profits very quickly and often several times each day. Another big difference is that the day trader is usually happy regardless of whether a market goes up or down, since he can make money in both directions.

◆ On the positive side, a successful day trader can enjoy a great deal of wealth, convenience and independence.

◆ On the negative side, day trading isn't easy. It requires a lot of study and the realisation that money can be lost - especially in the early months. It also requires a sufficiently equipped working space which provides access to stock prices, news and the ability to open and close positions at the touch of a button.

## Chapter Two

# How The Markets Work

> **Key Concept:**
> Market movements give people the opportunity to day trade.
> The purpose of this chapter is to examine how the markets
> work and what makes them move in the way they do.

One of the main reasons why day trading has become increasingly popular over recent years is because the stock markets of the world have become increasingly volatile. This increased volatility is what gives people the opportunity to open and close positions several times a day and still make good profits.

The stock market is, in theory, much like any other market. It's simply a place where buyers (of shares, options, commodities, etc.) meet with sellers and deals are made. So what factors make the stock markets move the way they do? There are three main factors which are generally said to be responsible:

- ◆ The general economic climate.
- ◆ The laws of supply and demand.
- ◆ The general mood of investors.

Each of these factors affect stock markets in different ways. To make these variable influences as easy as possible to understand, let us take a look at each one in turn...

## The General Economic Climate

This is, to put it simply, the state of the country we live in from a financial point of view. The general economic climate is affected by wars, rumours of wars, unemployment figures, interest rates, current or pending political elections, the size of the national debt and a whole host of other imponderables. Unfortunately, few people ever really seem to agree as to what is, or is not, good for the economy.

For example, if the rate of unemployment increases dramatically, one group of doom-and-gloomers will predict the arrival of a new depression or recession.

On the other hand, if the rate of unemployment decreases dramatically, another group of doom-and-gloomers will state that the economy is progressing too quickly and must be slowed down! So having said that, is unemployment good or bad for the economy? I'll let you decide that for yourself.

This state of affairs is something that invariably baffles the new investor. What you should remember is; what the majority of investors believe about the economical climate often affects share prices more than the economy itself. For example, if the majority of investors are optimistic, then more shares will be bought and stock markets will tend to rise. By the same token, if the majority of investors are pessimistic, then more shares will be sold and stock markets will tend to fall. This optimism and pessimism doesn't have to be based on any real economic data.

## The Laws of Supply and Demand

The laws of supply and demand are the same in the stock market as they are in any other type of market. If there is a high demand for a certain product and supply is limited then prices will tend to rise, but if there is little demand for a product then prices will tend to fall.

Demand for certain types of shares tends to rise or fall according to how the underlying company performs. The shares of an established company, which has good prospects for further growth or profitability, will naturally be in higher demand than those of a company which is relatively new and/or has few prospects.

As with the general economic climate, what investors believe about the prospects of a company can affect share prices as much, if not more than, any amount of hard data. Rumours that XYZ Cigarettes are to be successfully sued by a disgruntled smoker can send share prices plummeting because investors know that if the rumour is true, the cost of damages will affect the overall profitability of the company and open the floodgates for similar claims.

Similarly, rumours that ABC Avionics are about to be awarded with a mammoth contract from NASA can send share prices through the roof, simply because investors know that if the rumour is true profitability is sure to take an upward turn.

# The General Mood of Investors

We have already referred to the general mood of investors twice in the last few minutes, and it must be said that this is what generates the majority of market price fluctuations. Let's face it, if market prices were determined solely by hard economic or corporate data then they would be far more stable than they are in actuality. The fact that market prices often fluctuate wildly despite hard data is proof that emotion is king as far as the stock markets are concerned.

Emotions are impossible to quantify and even more difficult to predict, but a good idea of what the majority of investors think can be gained by paying close attention to the financial headlines in newspapers or on television news bulletins. These are the headlines which will be seen, read or heard by millions of investors – both private and professional – and undoubtedly have at least some effect on the direction the stock market takes.

To explain this situation, let us use the analogy of sheep and a shepherd. It is a rather crude analogy, but it sheds a great deal of light on the subject of share price fluctuations.

If you consider the masses of private investors to be sheep, and the financial media to be a shepherd, then it becomes clear that whichever direction the shepherd chooses to travel in, the sheep will surely follow.

Of course, there is always the odd black sheep who goes against the trend, but in the main mass-psychology will out and so financial headlines tend to become self-fulfilling prophecies.

For example, if a major financial journalist states that share prices are too high and will undoubtedly take a dramatic tumble in the near future, millions of sheep-like investors will take those words as gospel and act on them instinctively. They will sweat all night, call their brokers at first light and sell their holdings as quickly as possible. Supply drops off quite suddenly and, naturally, share prices do take the tumble that was predicted.

At this point everyone is sure that the financial journalist is a genius – if not a prophet – and so when he announces that the tumble is over and share prices are about to rocket, everyone piles back into the stock market. Demand soars, supply is limited and so share prices rise. The prophet scores two out or two for accuracy.

Because mass psychology has such a large effect on the stock market as a whole, patterns of rises, declines and crashes tend to repeat themselves quite dramatically over the long term. Certain patterns have been named and can be recognised quite readily when one knows what to look for.

Here are the "big three" patterns which all investors should be aware of.

## The Bull Market

A bull market is one in which share prices are on an upward trend. Share prices may dip for a day or week or month, but the underlying trend is upwards – often into new, uncharted territory. The illustration below shows the London FTSE 100 index during a bull run. Note how the price goes down as well as up, but the overall trend is positive.

## Bull Market

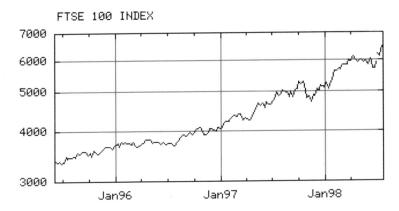

FTSE 100 INDEX

The average bull market lasts for around four years and general investing sentiment is usually quite positive.

Although some of the more pessimistic "gurus" of the investing world will warn of the impending down-trend which is "inevitable" even in the early months of a bull market, the majority of investors take confidence in the upward trend and continue buying shares even when hard data suggests that they are too expensive.

Towards the end of a bull market, share prices are much higher than they should be and news of rising interest rates will have begun to hit the headlines. At this stage even good news has little further positive effect on share prices.

# The Bear Market

A bear market is one in which share prices are on a downward trend. Share prices may rise for a day or week or month, but the underlying trend is undisputedly downwards. The illustration below shows the Japanese NIKKEI Index during a three-year bear market. Note how the price goes up as well as down, but the overall trend is negative.

## NIKKEI 225 INDEX

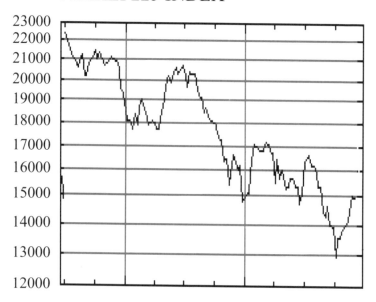

The average bear market lasts for around one year and general investing sentiment is usually quite negative. There is almost always talk from some quarters of the "inevitable" rise which lies just around the corner, but most investors avoid getting involved in the stock market through fear of suffering losses – even when hard data suggests that share prices are too low.

Towards the end of a bear market, share prices are much lower than they should be and interest rates may begin to fall. At this stage even bad news has little further negative effect on prices.

# The Crash

A crash is commonly defined as a sharp fall in general share prices which reduces the overall value of the stock market by ten per cent or more. This is more of an event than a trend, but it is suitable for discussion here because a crash tends to follow a definite pattern.

To begin with, a crash normally happens when the **vast majority** of the investment world least expects it. Markets will normally have been on an upward trend for quite some time on both sides of the Atlantic, often breaking into new, uncharted territory. During this time there will naturally have been some talk of how the market is due a "correction" of some kind. But, in the main, investor confidence will have been high. "This time things are different," many will say in response to the doom-and-gloomers.

And then, quite suddenly, the market suffers a massive drop. This could be due to bad economic news or some other event, but whatever sparks the initial fall in share prices, panic sets in and everyone heads for the exit. The phone lines to brokers become jammed as everyone desperately attempts to sell stock which no-one wants to buy, and the fall spirals rapidly.

# INVESTING FOR THE LONG TERM

How the UK FTSE 100 Share Index has performed since 1985

However disastrous a stock market crash might appear, historical data indicates that recovery comes *relatively* quickly. It took only two years to recover from the infamous stock market crash of 1987, and if you look at this event from a wider perspective of ten or even five years it is apparent that the crash was merely a large and necessary correction to stabilise what had been quite a dramatic upward trend.

Of course, a day trader who predicts a stock market correction or crash and decides to take advantage of it by purchasing put options or selling short can make a great deal of money if he is proved correct (assuming that legislation allows him to do this). And then, of course, he can ride the volatile waves up and down as the markets subsequently re-establish themselves. In short, large market corrections or even crashes aren't nearly as much of a nightmare for day traders as they sometimes are for traditional investors. In fact, they can be dreams come true.

## Predicting market movements

Because stock markets usually move according to the general economic climate, the law of supply-and-demand and the general mood of investors, they are usually more predictable than most people imagine. Generally speaking, most day traders predict market movements with something called **Technical Analysis.** This is the art of charting and interpreting historical share, commodity or market index figures in order to generate specific "up" or "down" signals which the trader then acts upon.

Technical analysis is really at the core of a day trader's ability to succeed. And because it is so important we will be discussing the subject in some depth later on in this book.

# Summary

◆ Stock markets move up or down due to three main factors: the current economic climate, the laws of supply and demand and the general mood of investors.

◆ Mass psychology often affects the fluctuation of stock markets as much – if not more so – than any other factor.

◆ Because mass psychology has such a large effect on the stock market as a whole, patterns of rises, declines and crashes tend to repeat themselves quite dramatically over the long term.

◆ A bull market is one in which share prices are on an upward trend. Share prices may dip from time to time, but the underlying trend is upwards. The average bull market lasts for around four years.

◆ A bear market is one in which share prices are on a downward trend. Share prices may rise from time to time, but the underlying trend is downwards. The average bear market lasts for around one year.

◆ A crash is commonly defined as a sharp fall in general share prices which reduces the overall value of the stock market by ten per cent or more. Historical data indicates that recovery from a crash usually comes relatively quickly.

## Chapter Three

# Setting Up
# as a Day Trader

> **Key Concept:**
> In order to work as a day trader, it is necessary to
> have a properly equipped office. This chapter details the
> bare bones of the modern day trader's set-up - from the
> computer to the all-important account with a broker.

It is the phenomenal evolution of computer and internet technology over the last couple of decades that has helped day trading to become as popular as it is today. For the first time ever, any man or woman who is so inclined can obtain all the equipment they need to day trade without taking out a second mortgage.

Of course, the most elaborate set-ups are very complex and therefore still costs a fairly substantial amount of money. But, as many people are discovering, almost all the technology needed to get started in day trading can be purchased on the High Street in a matter of hours.

In this chapter we will look at everything a beginner needs to commence day trading: from a quiet place to work right through to an actual account with a suitable broker. This "shopping list" of essentials is as follows...

# A Place to Work

Whilst you could possibly begin to day trade from your kitchen table, this is by no means recommended. One of the things you need to succeed in day trading is the ability to concentrate fully on what you are doing, and the kitchen table isn't usually conducive to that frame of mind. You will need to be free from distractions and interruptions - the kids fighting in the background could easily cause you to enter the wrong data into a spreadsheet or draw the wrong line on a chart.

So, if you seriously want to explore day trading for yourself you will need to set aside a whole room for the activity. This could be a spare bedroom or a custom-built home office. All that matters at this stage is that the room has a telephone outlet for internet connection and at least a couple of power points for your computer.

# The Computer

The personal computer is at the heart of any day trader's set-up. For the purpose of our discussion a modern personal computer can be divided into seven separate components. These are:

## Central Processing Unit (CPU)

The CPU is the "brain" of a personal computer, since it is responsible for processing all of the information it receives. The effectiveness of the CPU is generally gauged by the speed at which it operates, measured in Hertz (Hz), Megahertz (MHz) and Gigahertz (GHz). A computer which operates at 3.0Ghz (Gigahertz) will therefore be a lot more effective than one that operates at 2.0Ghz.

## Random Access Memory (RAM)

The RAM is the "short-term memory" of a personal computer. The more RAM a computer has, the more easily and efficiently it will be able to deal with the information it manages. RAM is measured in Kilobytes (K), Megabytes (MB) and Gigabytes (GB). For the record, one kilobyte of memory can hold 1,024 bits of information, one Megabyte is equal to 1,000K and one Gigabyte is equal to 1,000MB.

When personal computers were first introduced to the general public, Bill Gates, founder of Microsoft, commented that "640K of memory should be enough for anyone." Whilst this may have been true at the time, computer technology has advanced rapidly since the early days, and today you won't find many machines for sale with less than several GB of RAM as standard. Indeed, the amount of RAM that personal computers boast increases from year to year, so the rule of thumb here is to choose a machine with as much RAM you can afford.

## The Hard Disk

The hard disk is where the computer can permanently store information for future reference. Again, the larger the hard disk in terms of capacity, the better it is for the user. Hard disk capacity, like Random Access Memory, is measured in Megabytes and Gigabytes.

# Optical Disk Drive

An optical disc drive allows the computer to read and/or write information from and to optical media such as Compacts Discs (CDs) and Digital Versatile Discs (DVDs). The efficiency of an optical disc drive is gauged by its speed. The faster an optical drive can read and write information from and to the media, the better.

# The Monitor

The monitor is a visual display unit that presents images generated by the computer. Computer monitors have evolved at roughly the same rate as television screens, and so a modern monitor uses flat screen LCD technology as opposed to an old-fashioned cathode ray tube (CRT). This enables monitors to provide a large display without taking up an unacceptable amount of desk space. As far as the private investor is concerned, a huge display is generally unnecessary, so a fairly standard 19" screen is perfectly acceptable.

# Internet Capability

Having some kind of internet access is almost essential in the modern world, and buying a personal computer that is not 'internet-ready' is usually a false economy. The type of internet access you can get will depend to a great extent on your geographical location. Most people can be connected to the internet via a cable or broadband service, but in some cases a service that uses satellite technology might need to be employed instead. Whatever methods of internet access you have to choose from, you should opt for the fastest service possible. This will generally be the one with the highest bandwidth, measured in megabits per second (Mbps). A service offering 50Mbps would therefore be better than one offering 10Mbps.

## Back-up

You will need some method of saving your acquired data and research, and of backing up whichever work documents and programs you are using. There are several back-up methods that you can use, but the most popular options for day traders are as follows:

*USB Flash Drives* – These are USB devices that plug into your PC and allow you to save data to a flash memory unit. The main advantage of USB flash drives is that they are simple to use and as portable as you could hope for – simply back up your data, remove the USB device and put it in your pocket. The better USB flash drives can even secure your data with encryption and password protection.

*External Hard Drives* – The work exactly like regular hard drives, but they are external to your PC so you can plug them in, back up your data and then disconnect the external drive before putting it in a safe place. The big advantage of external hard drives is that they can hold a lot more data than USB flash drives, but they are obviously less portable.

*Virtual Drives* – These are internet-based services which allow you to back up your data to a remote server. You will need to pay a subscription fee on a monthly or annual basis, but when you're up and running backing up your data is as simple as uploading your essential files to your virtual drive. Virtual drives are extremely convenient, but whether you use them depends on how sensitive your data is and how secure it needs to be. For very important data the other two backup options would be preferable, if only because it makes sense to keep such data under your personal control at all times.

Now, although the actual components themselves (CPU, RAM, hard disk, optical disc drive, monitor and back-up device) will probably remain much the same for the foreseeable future, all of the above information is subject to change as technology continues to improve. You should therefore expect personal computers to become even faster and more efficient as the years roll by.

If you are looking for an order of preference, you could do worse than putting internet connection speed first, followed by RAM, CPU speed, Hard disk capacity, back-up facility, CD/DVD access speed and finally monitor size.

# The Software

Once you have a computer, you will need some software. The day trader generally needs several different types of software, or one professional package which can do everything. Whichever option is selected, the software a day trader uses will need to be able to perform the following functions:

## Data Retrieval

Because the prices of shares, commodity futures and market indices change throughout the day, you must be able to retrieve data on a regular basis from the internet.

The main way of doing this is to retrieve data from the internet.

There are a number of services available which will give you market data for free. However, that data will be delayed for a period, usually 20 minutes, which can make a big difference. While you are waiting for your data to come through, your fellow day traders will be happily selling or buying on the strength of a technical analysis signal. By the time you know a signal has been triggered, the price could have moved significantly.

To obtain 'real-time' data throughout the day will involve paying a fee to a service provider such as eSignal (www.esignal.com), but since this kind of information is vital to successful day trading, it must be considered an essential expense.

## Technical Analysis

Once you computer has retrieved market data, the next step is to analyse this data. Chapters 6 through 9 discuss technical analysis in detail because it is important that you understand how it works. The good news is, however, that your computer can do all of the hard number-crunching work for you pretty much automatically and produce moving averages, relative strength indicators, over-bought and over-sold signals and much, much more at the click of a mouse button.

## Optional : Automatic Signal Generation

Although this is not a prerequisite for successful day trading, many day traders use software which not only retrieves and analyses market data continuously, but also signals them every time it comes across a buy or sell signal.

Of course, this kind of software is top-of-the-range, both in terms of performance and cost, but if you are serious about becoming a successful day trader then the expense involved in acquiring such user friendly software will be more than justified by the time you save and the (hopefully profitable) signals it generates.

# The Trading Account

Now that you have a computer and software which allows you to retrieve data, analyse it and possibly even generate automatic buy and sell signals, the next step is to open an on-line trading account with a broker which you will use to open and close your positions via the internet.

Choosing a suitable on-line broker is largely a personal matter. If you already have a regular account with a broker, and this broker also offers on-line trading facilities, then you may well decide that staying with a company you know and trust is the wisest choice to make.

If you don't already have an account with a broker then you must, of course, shop around to find one that suits your needs. When researching on-line brokers, be sure to answer the follow-ing questions that will all help you to reach a sound decision:

## What charges and Commissions are Payable?

Because day trading is becoming increasingly popular, more and more brokers are competing to accommodate this trend. Comm-issions and charges therefore vary quite a lot between brokers, and high commissions don't always reflect a high standard of service. This being the case, it makes sense to consider carefully any on-line broker which offers lower commissions without sacrificing on quality of service.

# How Reliable is the On-line Trading Service?

Some on-line services are notoriously difficult to get through to during busy periods, and no day trader can afford to waste time when money is at stake. Positions need to be opened and closed as quickly as possible as soon as the day trader decides to do so. For this reason it is essential that you can rely on your on-line broker being available whenever you need to buy or sell.

# Is There a Telephone-Trading Back-up Service?

You may never need to use it, but your broker should have a telephone back-up system in place so that you can call him and provide instructions verbally. The obvious example of when this might be necessary is during an unexpected power cut, when your computer is, for all intents and purposes, temporarily redundant. In such a situation it is vitally important that you can call the broker on the phone and close any trading positions you may already have open.

# What support, if any, is offered?

Some on-line brokers offer the day trader free information, such as on-line charts, price histories and even tutorials on how to trade more effectively. These things aren't vital, but if you are torn between two brokers of equal reliability in all other respects, this kind of additional support can sometimes make all the difference.

When you have found an on-line broker you believe is most suitable for your day trading needs, opening an account is very easy.

You simply complete an application form, submit funds for your opening balance and then wait for your account to become active. Usually all of this can be done in the space of a week or so.

# The Library

As I said earlier (and I have no qualms about repeating myself since this is such an important point) this book is not designed to teach you all there is to know about day trading. It is written with the simple intention of providing you with an introductory grasp of the subject so that you can decide for yourself whether or not day trading is something you should investigate further. If you do decide that you would like to become a day trader then an essential part of your set-up will be a library of reference and text books. This library needn't take up the whole room, but it is important to have at least a few titles which go into a professional level of day trading detail - not only so that you have an initial working knowledge of how to trade effectively, but so that you can also refer to these texts whenever you need to remind yourself about specific day trading strategies, methods of chart interpret-ation and so on.

To start you off, there are three particular books which I strongly recommend to any aspiring day trader. These are:

| | |
|---|---|
| *Electronic Day Trading To Win* | *Bob Baird & Craig McBurney* |
| *The Complete Day Trader* | *Jake Bernstein* |
| *Electronic Day Trading 101* | *Sunny Harris* |

# A Filing System

Despite the fact that the vast majority of a day trader's work is done electronically via the Internet, day trading still generates a surprising amount of paperwork. Account statements, chart print-outs and so on should all be filed away in an organised manner. Not only will this make life as a day trader easier to cope with on a day to day basis, but it will also make sorting out tax affairs at the end of each financial year much less of a headache.

A filing system needn't be complex to begin with, and will naturally expand as your trading activities increase and become more evolved. In the early days a few simple box files will enable you to keep your paperwork in order and allow you to spend most of your time doing what day traders do best - day trading.
Okay, so you have a computer, software, an Internet connection, an account with a suitable broker, a simple reference library and a basis filing system. Does this mean that you're all set to start day trading?

Not yet, no. There are two more things you need. The first is an understanding of how to obtain general market information, and the second is a proper mindset which is so important to your success. We will discuss both of these requirements in the next two chapters...

# Summary

The bare bones of a day trader's "set-up" generally include the following:

♦ A **dedicated place to work.** Successful day trading requires concentration and focus, so a separate room for day trading purposes is recommended.

♦ A **computer**. The best you can afford. The bigger the capacity and speed of a computer, the better.

♦ An **internet connection.** A broadband connection should be considered the minimum.

♦ Appropriate **software.** A day trader needs software that can retrieve and analyse data throughout the day. He may also opt for a more evolved software package that generates automatic buy and sell signals.

♦ An **account** with an on-line broker so that the day trader can open and close positions via the Internet.

♦ A **library** of text books for initial study and future reference.

♦ A **filing system** so that the day trader can work in an organised manner

## Chapter Four

# Knowledge is Power

> **Key Concept:**
> Having a good knowledge of the current economic
> climate, breaking financial news and what other traders
> are doing all help to give the day trader the edge he needs
> to succeed more often than not. This chapter explains
> how such knowledge can be acquired -
> simply and effectively.

The difference between success and failure in any venture is often the quality of information at hand, and day trading is no exception to this general rule. The more you know about what is happening in the markets and why, the greater your chances of long-term success.

There are two main sources of financial information in the UK. The first is the financial press. The second is financial television programming. Let us look at each of these sources in turn.

## The Financial Press

Printed publications such as the Financial Times, the Investors Chronicle, and Shares magazine and online sources such as www. ft.com and www.iii.co.uk all contain a substantial amount of information that is of relevance to the day trader. Most day traders subscribe to several of these specialist titles and take the Financial Times as a matter of course.

If you decide to do the same, here are the main things to look at on a regular basis...

## The Headlines

It has already been said that the majority of investors are like sheep who act on herd instincts, buying or selling according to what everyone else is doing. The headlines in the financial press are one of the factors which affect this mass psychology in the first place - so you must pay attention to what they are saying.

It is obvious that not all headlines will agree, but again, the majority tends to rule. If seven out of ten headlines state that the stock market is heading for a crash then roughly seven out of ten people will believe this to be so and act on that belief as though it was a foregone conclusion. They will therefore tend to sell their shares rather than buy any more.

Conversely, if the majority of headlines predict a stock market boom then you might expect the majority of investors to be more interested in buying than in selling.

Studying the headlines of the financial press can help you gauge what the majority of investors will be thinking during any given period, and thus give you an insight into how the stock market will react.

# Share Prices

The prices of specific shares are central statistics which no day trader can afford to ignore. Of course, your computer and software package will enable you to retrieve data of this kind throughout the day, but it is also good to routinely browse through the price pages of any publication to ensure that you don't miss something of note.

Typically, shares are listed in groups, according to which sector of the market they are associated with. For example, television broadcasting companies and record companies tend to be listed under a heading such as "MEDIA" whilst computer manufacturing companies and retailers tend to be listed under "ELECTRICALS" or something similar. Knowing this can help you find the shares you are interested in quickly without having to wade through pages of listings.

The share details themselves normally comprise of at least five components, which are:

◆   The name of the company issuing the shares.
◆   The current share price.
◆   The change from the previous trading day.
◆   The share price high.
◆   The share price low.

This data might be set out as follows:

|  | Price | Change | Hi | Lo |
|---|---|---|---|---|
| **Invisible Widgets** | 303 | +7 | 303 | 270 |

This would mean that:

1. The ordinary shares issued by a company called Invisible Widgets stand at 303p each. This is the mid-price, so if you were to buy these shares they may actually cost a little more (say 305p), and if you were to sell them you may get back a little less (say 301p). Share prices given in any publication are for informational purposes only, and errors and omissions do occur, so you must always check the prices with your broker before buying or selling.

2. The next item of data tells you that the shares rose by 7p on the day. This means that the previous day's closing mid-price must have been 296p per share.

3. The third item tells you that the highest the shares have been is 303p per share. So Invisible Widgets' shares are currently trading at their highest level.

4. The final item tells you that the lowest the shares have been is 270p per share.

Sometimes other data is given, such as the **open**, day **hi** and day **lo** figures. These are simply the prices of the shares when the market opened and at the highest and lowest points on a particular day.

## Investment Tips

Almost every newspaper prints investment "tips" of one kind or another. These are buy or sell suggestions for certain shares and attract a massive following despite the fact that they are not to be construed as financial advice in the real sense of the phrase. Indeed, so many people follow the investment tips of particular publications that they too can tend to become self-fulfilling prophecies.

For example, if a tip is published in a popular Sunday newspaper to buy shares in Ocepoc Media Plc, millions of people will read that tip and thousands will act on it. The number of people who actually buy the shares will depend largely on how much the tipster is respected by the investing public. But you can be fairly sure that the share price will rise, at least for a short time, simply because of all the new buyers which the tip has generated. Similarly, a sell tip can cause the price of the share in question to fall over the next day or two.

Knowing what has been tipped as a buy or sell in the financial pages can be worth its weight in gold to the day trader who aims to generate profits by predicting share price movements. In many cases a day trader can make good profits simply by purchasing call options on "buy" tips and buying put options on "sell" tips. You should be aware however, that in order to do this effectively you need to act quickly. You should also note that tips alone don't guarantee the movement of any share - they only make movement more probable.

## Director Dealings

It makes sense that the people who are intimately involved with a particular company are likely to know more about it than the average investor. For this reason, many publications print a list of the most notable "Director Dealings". These are the shares bought or sold by directors of the company in question, and they reveal whether the people actually running the company are happy to increase their investment in it or are looking to reduce their holdings.

### Director Dealings   Ocepoc Plc   £350,000

Here, £350,000 has been invested by the director(s) in our fictitious company Ocepoc Plc. To many investors this is a significant transaction and could suggest that the director knows something that they don't in order to warrant such a large investment. Some private investors will therefore take a closer look at this company with a view to jumping aboard the band wagon and getting a slice of the action themselves.

Note the phrase, "a closer look" in that last paragraph. To day trade shares based solely on director dealings would be foolish. The sale or purchase may, for example, have been made purely on the grounds of the director's personal tax situation. However, such dealings, whether they are positive or negative, can and should be followed up with further study of the company in question. If this study concludes that the shares are indeed worth buying or selling on the basis of technical analysis, then the day trader can act on this informed opinion.

### Results Due
Almost all financial publications print a list of companies which are due to publish their final (annual) or interim (usually six monthly) accounts. Sometimes they also include an estimate of how much they think the Earnings Per Share (EPS) are likely to be.

Knowing which companies are due to publish their results is, in itself, important. Unless the results are **exactly** in line with expectations (of investors, not of the company involved), then there will be a price movement. The day trader, therefore, needs to be ready to react and have an idea which way the market will sway depending on the result.

Say Ocepoc PLC announced profits of £150 million, up from £120 million last year. On the face of things, you might expect the shares to rise. So you could buy the shares or call options. However, if the market had been expecting a rise in profits to £180 million, and they've come in short, you will probably see the shares drop and you should be selling or buying put options.

The schedule of pending results should also be read in conjunction with the table of Director Dealings. The smart day trader can often put two and two together and come up trumps. For example, if you have noted that a director of Ocepoc Plc has purchased £350,000 worth of shares in the last week, and that this company is due to publish its annual results soon, you might conclude that good news is on the horizon. This might explain why the director has made such a large investment, because, if the results are good, he knows that the world and his dog will want to buy shares in the company, thus pushing the price up. By purchasing £350,000 of shares before the publication of the results, they can benefit from this increase in share price almost automatically (even though, in theory, many may be restricted in the trading they can do in the run up to publication of results).

Of course, if the director had sold £350,000 of shares, then you might conclude that the results may not be very good. In this case it is likely that the director has sold his shares because he thinks they will soon go down in value.

Again, you are dealing here with clues to, not promises of, what might happen in the future. It is always advisable to check your technical analysis indicators before making a final decision to trade or not to trade in that particular company.

# Financial Television Programming

The two main sources of financial television programming, Bloomberg and CNBC, are supplemented by several second liners that vary according to the television networks operating in various countries. These channels are available to anyone capable of receiving satellite or cable prog-ramming, with CNBC coming out as the day trader's favourite - especially since they began broadcasting live prices presented in a constant "ticker" format across the bottom of the screen.

Both channels enable the day trader to keep his knowledge of the markets as current as is humanly possible. They tell the viewer not only what is happening, but also why it is happening and this latter information can be of great use when day trading since it can also indicate how long a particular trend is likely to last.

Another good thing about these channels is that they provide the day trader with information about the underlying pre-market sentiment among institutional traders. For example, before the American markets on one particularly memorable day, CNBC reported that many institutional traders were worried about the strong decline of the NASDAQ index having a very negative effect on the DOW JONES. Five minutes after opening, the DOW was down 100 points. At the end of the trading day it had lost over 600 points, and my guess is that I wasn't the only person to make a lot of money on this dramatic plunge.

Most day traders equip their home offices with a satellite or cable-fed television specifically so that they can make use of the CNBC or Bloomberg channels constantly as they work. This may cost a little more in the early days to pay for an extra television set and satellite or cable feed, but I for one think it is money very well spent.

# Knowledge is power
# – or is it?

In this chapter I have concentrated on explaining where a good current knowledge of the markets can be found, but it is important to remember that knowledge alone does nothing. In order to turn knowledge into day trading profits you must learn to use it properly. This is something that is learned "on the job" of day trading and cannot be gained solely from a text book. I can assure you however, that acquiring knowledge through the financial press and financial television programming will always help you to make better day trading decisions.

# Summary

♦ The financial press is a valuable source of information that no serious or aspiring investor can afford to overlook.

♦ Headlines in the financial press are one of the factors that affect the mass psychology of investors, so you must pay attention to what they are saying.

♦ Investment tips are followed by thousands of people and, at the very least, can often be seen as self-fulfilling prophecies.

♦ Director Dealings are printed in most financial publications and these can give you some insight as to what may lie in store for a company - particularly if they are studied in conjunction with a Results Due table.

♦ Both the CNBC and Bloomberg financial television channels can provide the day trader with an enormous amount of valuable information. For this reason many day traders ensure that their home office is equipped to receive these channels, even though doing so costs a little more in the early days.

**Chapter Five**

# The Mind-Set of Success

> **Key Concept:**
> The success or failure of a day trader can often be attributed to mental attitudes. This chapter details the mind-set of day trading success.

Although all successful day traders have skill and knowledge, that isn't all that is required to achieve success. There are many day traders who have a great knowledge of the markets but fail miserably when it comes to applying that understanding properly and profitably. What then, above knowledge and skill, determines the success or failure of a day trader? The answer is the mind-set.

Successful day traders tend to have what could be called "the mindset of success". This is simply a specific set of attitudes, beliefs and habits which enable them to make the most of their knowledge and skill and, therefore, to succeed in making consistent profits from their day trading activities.

Researchers have identified no less than ten traits which they believe make up "the mind-set of success" in the world of day trading. If you want to become a successful day trader then it is strongly suggested that you make these traits your own. The ten traits can be defined as follows:

# Have a Goal

It's no good becoming a day trader just because you want "to be successful in life." That aim is so vague and fuzzy that you will never know when you have achieved it.

Before you start day trading it is vitally important that you know why you want to be a day trader in the first place. Is it simply because you want to make more money? If so (and it usually is), how much money do you want to make? What will you do when you have this amount? Will you quit day trading or will you continue? And why?

A life without a goal is like a ship without a rudder. You might feel fine to begin with, being caught up in the excitement of opening and closing positions, but eventually you will realise that day trading has become just another job to you.

All businesses are a means to an end, and day trading is no different. Few people want to be day traders just for the sake of it. There has to be an ultimate aim - an underlying goal. That goal could be to retire with £500,000 in the bank at age 40. It could be to provide you with the freedom to take three days off each week to play golf.

Whatever the goal is, you need to know it before you get started. When you know what you want from day trading, write that goal down and refer to it at least once each week. That way, you'll always know whether or not your day trading is helping you to achieve it, and the real motivation for you being involved in day trading will never be far from your mind.

### *Be Patient*

Understand that although success can come swiftly to a day trader, it usually comes gradually. It is far more common for a day trader to earn £50,000 a year by making, say, 300 winning trades than it is for a day trader to make two winning trades worth £25,000 each.

In the beginning then, don't expect to become rich overnight. Day trading is not a get-rich-quick opportunity. It is a get-rich-slow opportunity. Be patient, concentrate on making a daily profit, however small, and the rest will take care of itself.

### *Be Positive*

A successful day trader is always positive. They are positive about their abilities, their strategies and they are positive in their outlook. Seldom does the professional day trader spend vast amounts of time moping over a loss or two. Instead they realise that losses are part of the day trading life, and that tomorrow there will be plenty of new opportunities to make winning trades.

### *Be Wise*

A day trader never risks more than he can afford to lose in a worse case scenario. Instead he is wise about the money he can afford to use for day trading purposes and should that money ever be depleted he knows he won't starve to death.

Most day traders also have money in more traditional long-term investment programmes such as bonds, mutual funds and so on. The money the wise man sets aside for day trading purposes is risk capital - pure and simple.

## *Specialise*

No successful day trader opens and closes positions across the board, getting involved in shares, commodity futures and market indices as the fancy takes him. Such a broad canvas makes long-term success very difficult indeed.

Successful day traders tend to specialise. Some restrict their day trading activities to certain sectors of the stock market, such as banking or bio-tech stocks. Others specialise in pork bellies and corn futures. Still others concentrate solely on trading index options.

Specialising in a certain kind of day trading enables the individual to develop a great knowledge of his chosen subject. He learns to anticipate the characteristic dips and rallies of his particular sector, and this in and of itself enables him to become more successful in generating end of day profits.

## *Be Disciplined*

One of the greatest keys to success in day trading is the ability to be disciplined. Many day traders fail because they don't do what they know they should do in order to succeed. Instead of disciplining themselves to stay out of a market when the charts suggest caution, they give in to gut feelings and end up losing money. Instead of executing a stop loss to limit the effect of a bad trade, their lack of discipline leads them to "hold on for a while longer" and lose more than they should.

An undisciplined day trader is, for all intents and purposes, a pure gambler. And as I said earlier in this book, gamblers will always lose in the long run. The rule of thumb therefore, is to be disciplined. Know what you should do in any situation and then do it. If you don't then you are setting yourself up to fail.

## Be Consistent

Consistency is closely related to self-discipline. To succeed as a day trader you need to be consistent from day to day. Don't use one strategy one day and another strategy on the next. Don't focus on index options today and then turn your attention to pork belly futures tomorrow. Instead decide what you are going to specialise in, decide what strategies are of most use to you and then be consistent with these decisions.

Note that being consistent doesn't mean that you can never change your approach, quite the opposite. By being consistent you will be able to identify what is going right and what isn't. If you had a more haphazard approach then you would never be sure why one trade will have worked out fine and another has resulted in a loss. So, a period of consistently applying your strategy will allow you to improve it and develop an even better strategy. Again, once you have the new strategy worked out, you will need to apply that consistently as well.

## Be Detached

If you get too emotionally involved in your trading activities you are asking for an ulcer. Of course day trading is exciting. Markets can swing up and down all day long. But if you aren't careful, you may find that your moods swing up and down with the markets, and this doesn't bode well for making good trading decisions.

It is difficult, but aim to be as emotionally detached as you can be whilst trading. This will not only keep any stress you experience to a minimum, thus preserving your health, but it will also enable you to make better trades.

### Be Grounded

Don't allow day trading to take over your entire life. Of course a successful trader thinks about day trading a good deal of the time, but it isn't the be all and end all of his existence, and it shouldn't be yours.

Make it a habit to spend at least an hour each day doing something totally unrelated to day trading. Go swimming, take a long walk, play golf, take your kids to the park. Do anything that will ground you in reality and give your mind some freedom from thoughts of day trading. Paradoxically, you will find that doing this will make you a better day trader than you would be if you thought about it constantly.

### Don't Get Addicted

As well as taking an hour each day to get your mind off day trading, you should also schedule at least one week in every twelve to "get away from it all". Some traders don't do this, and as a result they become addicted to day trading just as a junkie gets addicted to heroine. This is bad news, for it means that day trading is no longer an enjoyable way of achieving a goal or set of goals, but that it has instead become the meaning for their very existence.

There are successful day traders who trade every day without ever taking a break, and it can't be denied that some of these traders are incredibly wealthy. But that kind of wealth is pretty meaningless, since they never take time off to enjoy it anyway.

By all means, throw yourself into day trading. Enjoy it. Love it. But don't sacrifice the rest of your life for it. At the end of the day, day trading is just a new way of making money.

Adopt these ten traits as your own, live by their rules and when taken together with adequate knowledge and skill they will enable you to stand the greatest chance possible of success as a day trader.

# Summary

To succeed as a day trader, you need to adopt ten traits that comprise "the mind-set of success." The ten traits are as follows:

- Have a goal
- Be positive
- Be wise
- Specialise
- Be disciplined
- Be consistent
- Be detached
- Be grounded
- Don't get addicted

## Chapter Six

# Trading Strategies

## Part I

Key Concept:
Trend Lines and Channels are used by day traders to identify the broad movements of a particular market, share or commodity.

The following four chapters present various technical analysis techniques and strategies which are used by day traders to predict market movements. The information in these chapters is by no means exhaustive, but it should provide you with an overview of the strategies which day traders employ to help them make their trading decisions. They have been drawn from "*Timing the Financial Markets*" by Alex Kiam.

## Trend Lines

Literally hundreds of years of price charts bear testament to the fact that the values put on financial instruments tend to move in trends. These trends are simply indicators of an imbalance of supply and demand of a particular instrument. When the supply of an instrument is greater than the demand there will be more sellers than buyers, and the trend will be downwards. On the other hand, when demand exceeds supply, there will be more buyers and the price trend will be upwards. Should supply and demand be roughly equal, then the market will move sideways, not producing a discernible up or downtrend, and the price of the instrument will stay within a "trading range".

There are three forms of trend:

◆ **Minor Trends -**
  Are very short lived and lasts for only a few days to a couple of weeks,

◆ **Intermediate Trends -**
  Lasts for a few weeks to a couple of months

◆ **Major Trends -**
  Lasts for a period in excess of a couple of months and could be several years.

Once a trend comes to an end, then the trend that was apparent is usually reversed. So if a downtrend line is broken then it becomes a signal to buy. Similarly if an uptrend line is broken it is a signal to sell. This is made more obvious if you consider the underlying supply and demand. As discussed above the down-ward trend is caused by there being more sellers than buyers of a particular instrument in the market. If that trend comes to an end then you can surmise that there is no longer a surplus of sellers. Therefore the buyers are gaining an upper hand and the price will be expected to rise.

# Simple Trend Lines

An uptrend line or rising trend is defined by successively higher prices for a financial instrument, with the bulls being firmly in control. There will, of course, be small oscillations in the price throughout the period of the "uptrend". But each time the price drops slightly, due to a small correction such as profit taking, the "bottom" will be higher than the previous.

So on a chart of price against time you can draw a line connecting the successive bottoms as shown in Figure 6-1.

*Figure 6-1 An uptrend in Siebe shares*

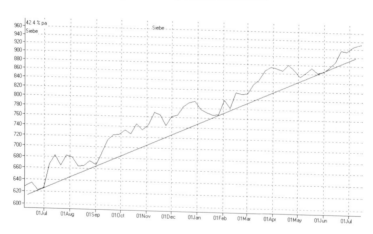

A falling trend line or **downtrend**, is defined by successively lower prices where the buyers are in control, pushing prices lower. This time the trend line is drawn across the "tops" of the falling price. So long the prices remain below or on this line the downtrend is in force - as show in Figure 6-2, overleaf.

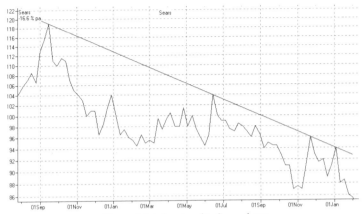

*Figure 6-2 A downtrend in Sears shares*

Technical analysts tend to talk about the **"authority"** or **"validity"** of the trend line. This depends on a number of factors including the number of bottoms or tops which have formed on the trend line, duration of the trend line, and the angle of the line drawn on the chart. A trend line which has a shallower angle in either direction, contains lots of bottoms or tops, and has been followed for a long time will be technically **"significant"** and carry a lot of "authority". A very steep trend line, on the other hand, exhibiting only two or three bottoms or tops and lasting for a short period is not very authoritative and is of less technical significance. In short, the more often that prices move in such a way to test the trend line (come close to or onto the line) and the trend holds, then the more authority it will have.

The start of a trend is difficult to spot because at the beginning you will only have one top or bottom to work with. So you will have to wait for prices to move in either direction and then react

again before you will get a second top or bottom. As soon as this
happens you can draw a line on your chart, though you already
know this will not have much authority. As time goes on another
top or bottom will be formed which may confirm your trend. With
just three points to work on (tops or bottoms) an exact trend will
have more authority. However it is more likely that these tops or
bottoms will not be exactly in line. At this point it will be possible
to draw two lines on your chart. The first will be drawn from your
first top or bottom to the second top or bottom, and the second
from your first top or bottom to your third top or bottom. The next
top or bottom that occurs will confirm which trend is in force and
will give it much more authority.

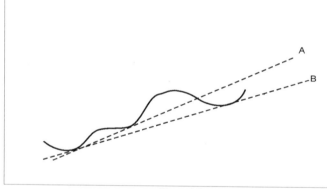

*Figure 6-3a*

Figure 6-3a shows this in operation in a rising market. Three
bottoms have been generated but it is possible to draw two lines,
**A** and **B**, across the bottoms of the data. At this point you don't
know which trend is going to take hold. Progressing to Figure 6-3b,
overleaf, you can see that another top and bottom has been created on
the chart and that a trend line with more authority can now be
drawn.

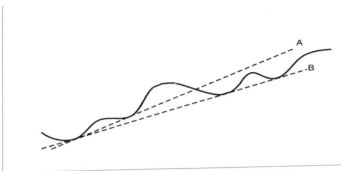

*Figure 6-3b*

If, when progressing from 6-3a to 6-3b the next bottom had not fallen as a point consistent with trends **A** or **B** then you would have had to have drawn a third line, **C**, shown in Figure 6-3c. When you get three lines on a chart like this they are known as **"fan lines"** and they indicate that a change is taking place. The general rule of thumb is that when a third fan line has been broken by the data then a trend direction will be reversed. So from Figure 6-3c you can expect a generally uptrending market to turn into a

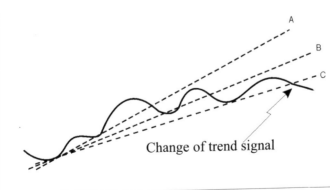

Change of trend signal

*Figure 6-3c*

downtrend. Similarly a series of downtrends in a falling market will be reversed into an uptrend by such a break.

# Penetrations

Never lose sight of the fact that technical analysis is not an exact science. The instant a trend line is broken you should refrain from diving into the market and committing a lot of money. Instead you should ask yourself some questions about the validity of the penetration and then make a qualified judgement as to how convincing it is. If the penetration was only minor then it must remain questionable and you should look at other factors.

For example, was the volume higher or lower on the day that penetration occurred? If volume was up then there is a good chance that the break is authentic. But if volume was down then the penetration remains questionable. You can also check to see if penetration occurred after a short period of sideways movement. If it did then this is more likely to be a testing of the trend line and the price could move in either direction. Here you would have to wait for more data before you could draw a definitive conclusion. Finally you could look for the penetration being accompanied by a reversal pattern which will be covered in Chapter 7.

Even when penetration is convincing you should refrain from committing large amounts of funds on a hunch that the opposite trend will take hold. Take this situation, for example, which is known as a **"pullback"**. The price of your shares have been moving on a steady uptrend for several hours and then you notice a sharp fall in prices which decisively penetrate the uptrend. After this significant fall there is a brief rally in the value of the shares taking the price back up briefly. The bottom that has been created is off the trend line and shows that it has been broken. However before the price starts to fall again a top is created which is actually higher than the price at which the trend line was broken. If you had gone short as soon as the penetration had taken place you could be looking at a loss within a few minutes or hours.

*Figure 6-3d*

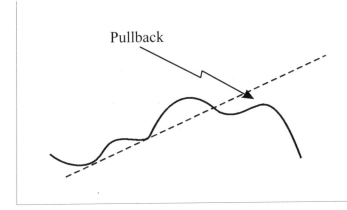

Of course, if you wait for the pullback before you go short in order to maximise your profit then you run the risk that it will never occur and you end up selling short at a disadvantageous price. Some analyst's advocate taking up half of your short position as soon as the trend line is broken and the other half when the pull back occurs. However I prefer to work to the penetration of the trend line and if I lose a little bit of extra profit by the occurrence of a pull back, then so be it. Greed has been the downfall of many an investor and I am a great believer in *"leaving a bit of profit for the next man"*.

# Trend Channels

When an authoritative trend is occurring it is possible to draw a second line on your charts parallel to the original trend line. This second line is drawn so that it touches the opposite feature of the price oscillation. So for an uptrend you have already drawn a line through successive bottoms. On this chart your parallel line will be drawn so that it touches a couple of tops from the same rising trend. On a downtrend the original line is drawn touching successive tops so the parallel line is made to touch the corresponding bottoms.

This second line is usually called the **"return line"** because it marks a point at which a price is about to return towards the trend line. The area between the original trend line and the new return line is known as the **"trend channel"** - see Figure 6-4a.

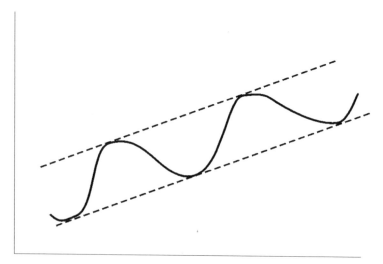

*Figure 6-4a*

Obviously a trend is a money making opportunity in itself. When an uptrend is in force simply buy the financial instrument in question and as long as the prices follow the trend you will be making profit. Similarly if you sell or go short in an instrument that is on a downtrend, and then close your position out when penetration occurs, you also make a profit. However, it is possible to increase the amount of money that you make during a trend by taking advantage of the price oscillations along the way. And this is where the trend channel is most useful.

Take your chart showing your trend channel and now draw a third line parallel to and midway between your existing two lines. You have now split your channel into "two zones". The upper zone is called the **"sell zone"** and when the price enters this area you should sell the instrument. The lower zone is called the **"buy zone"** and you should buy whenever the price comes into the zone. Of course the price volatility needs to create a sufficiently

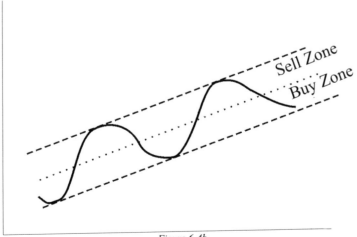

*Figure 6-4b*

wide channel for you to be able to make a profit once you have taken dealing costs into consideration.

One further use of the return line is that it can be used as a warning signal and alert you to the fact that a trend may soon be broken. If a price regularly oscillates between the basic trend and the return line, but then fails to rise as high or fall down to the return line, then you should be aware that penetration may occur next time the prices approach the original trend line.

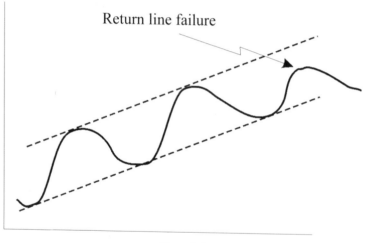

Return line failure

*Figure 6-5*

## Volume

The volume, or number of shares or contracts that change hands in a given day, is an important indicator to technical analysts. This is because a large volume adds authority to any price simply because it is a consensus between a lot more people.

As you know trends are created by an imbalance of supply and de-mand. When prices are rising there is more demand than supply, and when prices are falling there is more supply than demand.

So to fit in with the use of volume as a gauge of the market the volume that coincides with a price increase is known as **"demand volume"** and the volume that occurs during a fall is known as **"supply volume"**.

If you think about the situation logically you will come to the conclusion that you need increasing volume for prices to go higher. If there are lots of sellers of a financial instrument, or any other product for that matter, but no buyers, then no deals can be struck and the volume will be zero. But as soon as suppliers appear and a price can be agreed, some deals will be struck, and volume will be created. As more buyers come along and volume increases there will be a relative scarcity of the stock that they want - so prices will start to increase.

Based around this you can create five basic rules for using volume analysis in conjunction with your trend lines:

◆ When prices are going up and the volume is increasing then the trend will stay in force and prices will continue to rise.

◆ When prices are going up and the volume is decreasing the trend is unlikely to continue and prices will either increase at a slower rate or start to fall.

◆ When prices are decreasing and volume is increasing then the trend will continue and prices will fall further.

♦ When prices are decreasing and the volume is also decreasing then the trend is unlikely to continue and the decline in prices will slow down or they will start to increase.

♦ When volume is consistent, not rising or falling, then the effect on prices is neutral and you need to find some other way of backing up your trend analysis.

# Summary

♦ The values put on financial instruments tend to move in trends. These trends are simply indicators of an imbalance of supply and demand.

♦ Minor Trends are very short lived and last for only a few days to a couple of weeks,

♦ Intermediate Trends last for a few weeks to a couple of months,

♦ Major Trends last for a period in excess of a couple of months and could be several years.

♦ The volume, or number of shares or contracts that change hands in a given day, is an important indicator to technical analysts.

♦ Never lose sight of the fact that technical analysis is not an exact science. The instant a trend line is broken you should refrain from diving into the market and committing a lot of money. Instead you should ask yourself some questions about the validity of the penetration and then make a qualified judgement as to how convincing it is.

| Price | Volume | Trend |
|:-----:|:------:|:-----:|
| ↑ | ↑ | ↑ |
| ↑ | ↓ | → oρ ↓ |
| ↓ | ↑ | ↓ |
| ↓ | ↓ | → oρ ↑ |
| → | n/a | |

## Chapter Seven

# Trading Strategies

## Part II

> **Key Concept:**
> Reversal patterns are used by the day trader to help predict the end of a trend.

Whenever a price trend is in force, be it upwards or downwards, at some point it will come to an end. You could say there are actually three things that are certain in life: **death, taxes and the end of trends!**

The problem comes in predicting, exactly, when an uptrend or a downtrend or a sideways movement is going to come to an end. A technical analyst has many tools at his disposal to help him in his search for the end of a trend, but one of the most powerful is the presence of a **"reversal pattern"**.

These reversal patterns take the form of a characteristic shape on a chart and serve to give you an indication of which direction the market is going to move in, rather like patterns of stars were used by ancient mariners to navigate the seas. As you become more experienced in technical analysis you will learn to recognise the following patterns without a second thought:

- ◆ Head and shoulders top & bottom
- ◆ Double top & bottom
- ◆ Triple top & bottom
- ◆ Rounding top & bottom
- ◆ Broadening formation
- ◆ Rising and falling wedge

# Head and Shoulders Top

You will find that this formation is a common characteristic of many share price charts, and is one of the most reliable forms of reversal pattern. As it's name implies, the shape consists of a left shoulder followed by a head and then a right shoulder.

The **left shoulder** is formed at the end of an extensive increase in price where the volume associated with it has been quite high. The shoulder rounds as the price dips slightly quite typically on lower volume. This dip is the start of the **neckline** and the head is about to form.

The **head** is then formed with associated heavy volume on the rising part of the head and less volume on the falling part. Prices then fall to somewhere near the same level as the low of the left shoulder.

It does not have to be at exactly the same level and could be slightly higher or lower, but definitely below the top of the left shoulder.

All is set for the **right shoulder** to be formed by a rally in the price to a level roughly equal with that of the left shoulder. Again it can be slightly higher or lower but definitely below the high achieved by the head. The volume associated with this rally will usually be less than the rallies which formed the left shoulder and the head.

Once the right shoulder has started to form you can draw in a "neckline" across the bottoms created between the left and head and the head and right shoulder. Once the price falls from the right shoulder and breaks through the neckline the Head and Shoulders Top formation has been confirmed and it is your signal to go short in that particular financial instrument.

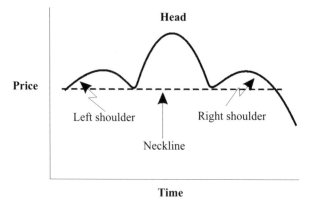

*Figure 7-1*

Quite often, once the neckline has been broken, you will see that prices will pull back towards the neckline before falling away sharply. This is similar to a "trader's remorse" period with the neckline acting as a resistance level instead of a mini support level during the Head and Shoulders Top formation. Keep a close eye on prices during this remorse period and be prepared to react in case it turns into a bull trap.

As indicated above the Head and Shoulders Top formation does not need to be perfectly symmetrical. The time taken to create each of the shoulders may be different. This will cause one shoulder to look slightly larger than the other even though it has reached a similar high point. Also the neckline does not have to be exactly level and may slope up or down. This will make one of the shoulders look as though it is drooping or that the head is lopsided. Notice here, however, that it is important that the lowest point on the right shoulder must be lower than the highest point on the left shoulder, otherwise you may simply have an uptrend that is changing it's gradient.

# Head and Shoulders Bottom

This is quite obviously the opposite of a head and shoulders top! It usually accompanies a reversal from a downtrend to one which is in the upwards direction. The main difference between this and the Head and Shoulders Top is in the volume pattern associated with the share price movements. The volume should pick up as the prices increase from the bottom of the head and then increase even more on the rally which follows the right shoulder. If the neckline is broken with an associated low volume then you should be sceptical about the validity of the formation.

# Double Top Formation

These appear in the shape of the letter M on a chart and are also common.

A Double Top, believe it or not, is rather like a Head and Shoulder Top formation but without the head! A peak price is reached before a small decline, which causes the valley between the Double Tops, and then the price rallies again to a peak roughly equal to the level of the first. The price then falls away on a new downtrend.

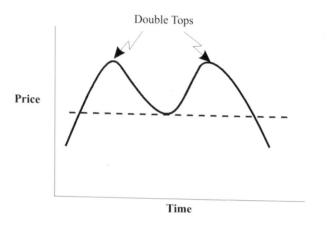

*Figure 7-2 A classic Double Top reversal*

The correct prediction of a true Double Top formation is more difficult than for a Head and Shoulder formation. This is because a simple uptrend, with each new wave of buying interspersed with minor reactions and profit taking, will appear as if it is making a Double Top formation. However, as you can see in Figure 7-3, the data can progress in either direction.

Once you reach the point shown by the end of the continuous line shown on Figure 7-3 you cannot be sure if the Double Top formation will be confirmed and the price will drop away, or if the price will again rally and the uptrend will stay in force. In roughly

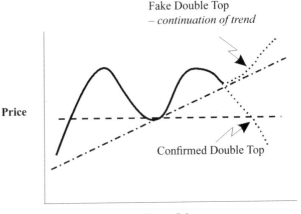

*Figure 7-3.*

90% of cases you will find that the Double Top is, indeed, a fake in the making and the uptrend will stay in force.

Volume is, yet again, your best friend in determining whether a true Double Top formation is being created or if it is going to be a fake. Look at the volumes associated with both of the peaks. If the volume associated with the first peak is greater than that associated with the second peak then this is an indicator that the prices will fail to go higher - confirming the Double Top formation. If the volume accompanying the second rise is the same as that accompanying the first, or even greater, then it is likely that the uptrend will be continuing.

The time span taken to create the Double Top formation is another factor which can help you determine the likely progression of the price data. If the two tops are fairly close together in terms of time then you should suspect that it is merely a consolidation period, a pause for breath, before the rally continues. But if the peaks are separated over a longer period and the valley between the two peaks is fairly deep then you can be more sure that you are looking at a true Double Top.

# Double Bottom

This is the opposite of a Double Top and appears as a letter W on a chart. The formation of a double bottom and the indicators of the reversal are very much the same as for a Double Top. However the volume patterns are very different. This time a true double bottom formation will show increased volume on the rally up from the second bottom over the rally from the first bottom. If the volume associated with the rally from the second bottom is less than or equal to the volume associated with the rally from the first bottom, then you are probably looking at a pause in a continuing downtrend.

# Triple Tops and Bottoms

These are a fairly rare species and you will not see them on many charts. As with the Head and Shoulders formation and the Double Top, the peaks and troughs do not have to be equally spaced. Nor do the peaks or the troughs have to reach the same levels or bottom out at exactly the same price to form a valid formation.

The volume associated with the Triple Top needs to be progressive. So the volume associated with the first peak needs to be larger than that associated with the second peak, which is itself larger than that associated with the third. Note, however, that the true Triple Top formation is not confirmed until prices have finally broken through a level equal with the lower of the two troughs.

A problem occurs, of course, with the Triple Top at the Double Top stage! Once the Double Top has been confirmed (in other words you realise that the uptrend is not continuing) it would be valid to think that the price is going to drop away sharply.

However, the possibility remains that you are heading for a Triple Top. So a good trading strategy, if prices appear to be rallying slightly after a Double Top confirmation, is to go short in the market but to set a stop loss at a level equal to the highest peak of the Double Top formation.

# Rounding Tops and Bottoms

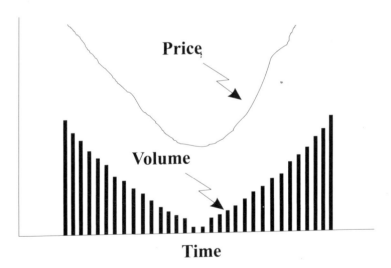

*Figure 7-4*

These appear to form an n or U shape on your chart and are hard to detect.

The way, yet again, to pick them out from a simple consolidation pattern is to look at the volume. In a true rounded bottom formation you will see that volume decreases as the price decreases, which signifies an easing of selling pressure. As the price movement becomes neutral and goes sideways you will see that there is very little trading activity and volumes are very low. Then, as prices start to increase, the volume will increase as well. The volumes and the prices, will now become almost a reflection of those which occurred during the decline.

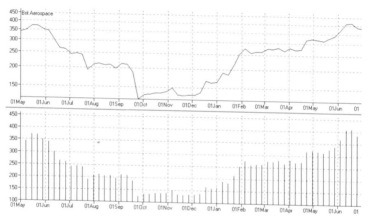

*Figure 7-5 A rounded bottom at British Aerospace*

# Broadening Formations

The theory behind this reversal pattern is that five smaller reversals are followed by a substantial change. An example is shown in Figure 7-6.

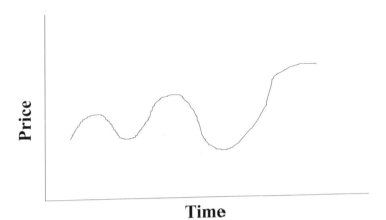

*Figure 7-6*

Note that "reversal" takes the literal meaning here and is a change of direction; so the five smaller reversals are changes from a falling market to a rising market, and a rising market to a falling market, and not five falls or five rises. Although the chart can be either way up, as a broadening tops or broadening bottoms reversal pattern, similar rules hold. Reversal three must occur at a higher level than reversal one, and reversal five, must be higher yet again. Also reversal four must occur at a lower level than reversal two (one, three and five must be successively lower, and two and four successively higher in the case of a broadening bottom).

The underlying idea behind this reversal pattern is that the market is almost out of control and lacking support from well-informed investors. The first reversal is supposedly created by "smart money" leaving the market, with the subsequent rises being attributed to an influx of the general public. Reversal number three is attributed to the smarter investors going short in stocks, whilst reversal five is, of course, the unavoidable drop. Volume is also erratic during this period and does not help with the interpretation of the charts.

Perhaps the best way to view this formation is as if the market is gradually becoming more and more unstable. As the swings get wilder and wilder something is going to break!

# Wedge Formations

These can appear as rising or falling wedges. If you were to draw your trend lines along the bottoms of a share price movement and along the top, as per Chapter 4, instead of forming a parallel uptrend channel, they will converge to form a triangle. If the triangle is pointing upwards, as in Figure 7-7, then a market fall can be expected after the price curve penetrates the lower line. If the triangle is pointing downwards (a falling wedge) then the market will rise once the upper line is penetrated. If the wedge or triangle is level, in other words not pointing up or down, then this is a "consolidation" pattern and you can expect the trends to continue.

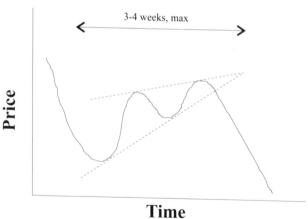

*Figure 7-7.*

You will notice on Figure 7-7 that a time period of 3-4 weeks across the entire formation has been marked. This is because wedge formations only occur as reversals of intermediate and minor trends. They will not be seen, except in unusual circumstances, as a reversal to a major market trend.

# Summary

◆ Reversal patterns take the form of a characteristic shape on a chart and serve to give you an indication of which direction the market is going to move in.

◆ There are six main patterns which, with practise, you will come to recognise. These patterns are known as:
  ● The head and shoulders top & bottom
  ● The double top & bottom
  ● The triple top & bottom
  ● The rounding top & bottom
  ● The broadening formation
  ● The rising and falling wedge

## Chapter Eight

# Advanced Trading Strategies

## Part I

> **Key Concept:**
> Moving averages are a day trader's best friend and enable
> them to determine the optimum times for opening and
> closing positions.

Moving averages are one of the oldest and most popular technical analysis tools particularly amongst day traders. The moving average is the average price of a financial instrument at a given time. And so when you are calculating the moving average you need to specify the "time span" over which the average is calculated.

A simple moving average is calculated by adding together the closing prices of a financial instrument over a certain number of time periods and then dividing the sum by the number of periods involved. So, for example, the seven-day average for a share price would be calculated by taking seven days worth of data, adding them together and dividing by seven. A seven-minute average would be calculated by taking seven minutes worth of data and doing the same.

Note that so far you have only calculated the seven-day (or minute) average of the share price and not the seven-day 'moving' average. To go on and calculate the moving average you need to have, in this example, at least eight days worth of data. You start it by taking the first seven days worth of data and calculating the average value. This is now your first point on the moving average curve. Once you have plotted this, return to your data and drop off the first or earliest data point from your original seven, leaving you with the six most recent values. Now add the latest piece of information to the six that you have been left with (in other words your eighth point) to give you a new set of seven. Take the average, again, of these new seven pieces of data (data points 2-8) to give you your second point on the moving average curve. The third

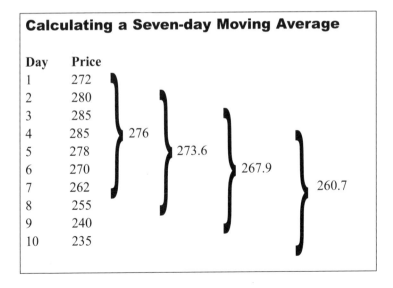

**Calculating a Seven-day Moving Average**

| Day | Price |
|-----|-------|
| 1   | 272   |
| 2   | 280   |
| 3   | 285   |
| 4   | 285   |
| 5   | 278   |
| 6   | 270   |
| 7   | 262   |
| 8   | 255   |
| 9   | 240   |
| 10  | 235   |

276
273.6
267.9
260.7

moving average point will be calculated by taking the average of data from points 3-9 inclusive, the fourth will be an average of 4-10 inclusive, etc.

Moving averages can be calculated for any period to give you short, medium and long-term views on the movement of a share price. The short-term average can be obtained by taking a five-day moving average (the number of working days in a week), the medium term by taking a 13-day average and a slightly longer term by taking a 20-day average. As the number of days in the moving average increases, then the moving average itself becomes smoother and less responsive to the short-term fluctuations in the market. It is therefore slower to respond to changes in any trend and will give you fewer "false starts". However, as with all things, what you gain on the swings you lose on the roundabouts, and you will find that a large slice of the price move has already taken place by the time a longer moving average has signalled a change.

It is possible to calculate other moving averages such as a "weighted" moving average where you give more significance to some data than to others. For example, you may wish to give the latest data in your set of prices more significance than the earlier data since it gives a better representation of current market thinking. A very crude way of achieving this would be to double the value of your last data point and then divide by the number of time periods plus one.

A more effective and popular way with serious technical analysts is to use a weighting factor known as exponential smoothing. This gradually gives more and more significance to the latest data and therefore the latest information to enter the market. A detailed discussion of exponential smoothing is beyond the scope of this book, but most technical analysis software packages are capable of implementing the technique at the push of a button.

The final point to address with moving averages is where you plot the "average point" that you calculated. Refer again to the seven-day moving average that we calculated above. The first moving average data point of 276 refers to days 1-7. Now when you come to plot it on your chart, along with the actual price data, where do you place it? You basically have two main options:

◆ Either plot it against day four (the middle of your data), or

◆ Plot it on day seven (the end of your data) which is known as a "lagging" moving average.

Most technical analysts opt for the latter of these and plot the lagging moving average. Figure 8-1, below, shows a chart of price

*Figure 8-1*

fluctuations for Glaxo Welcome shares along with a 20-day lagging moving average for the same data. Notice how peaks and troughs in the moving average data lag the same features in the actual price data

# Interpreting the Moving Average

The simplest way to interpret a moving average line is to depict a change of direction as a signal to buy or sell. So a moving average which changes from the 'increasing' or 'level' to 'decreasing' is a signal to sell, and one which changes from 'decreasing' or 'level' to 'increasing' is a signal to buy. All you have achieved with this form of interpretation is a smoothing of the basic price data, and it does not really offer you much advantage.

The classical interpretation, which is used by most technical analysts, is to use a moving average curve in conjunction with the underlying price movements. Most investors typically:

◆  Buy when a shares price rises above its moving average, and

◆  Sell when the shares price falls below its moving average.

Figure 8-2, overleaf, again shows basic price data for Glaxo Welcome shares along with the 20-day moving average, lagging. But this time the buy and sell signals have been marked on. You can see that this is clearly a powerful system and one that can be recommended for any budding technical analyst.

Using such a system ensures that you will always be on the correct side of the market and, as indicated before, you will experience fewer false starts. Indeed, a price cannot rise too

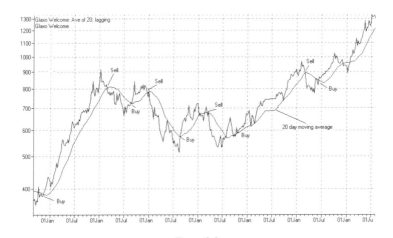

*Figure 8-2*

*Buy and sell signals from the 20-day moving*
*average of Glaxo Welcome shares.*

much without the underlying price rising above its average price.
But the main disadvantage is that you will always tend to buy and
sell late. You can see from Figure 8-2 that the actual point of the
buy and sell signals is a day or two after the underlying price has
started to fall or rise.

On balance, my personal view is that the pros of using this system
far out weight the cons. I would rather be on the right side of the
market, and leave a bit of profit for others, than try to squeeze
every single penny I can out of the market and end up taking a
hit.

One last thing to note with this classical interpretation is that the
change typically needs to last for a period around twice the length
of the moving average for you to make money once dealing costs
are taken into consideration.

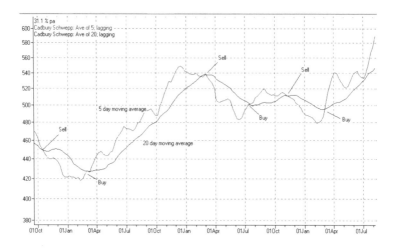

*Figure 8-3 Long and short moving averages give good buy and sell signals*

Perhaps a more powerful way of interpreting the data but slightly more complex than the one moving average, is to combine a short term moving average and a longer term moving average on the same chart. Figure 8-3 shows such a chart relating to shares in Cadbury Schweppes. Here you can see a five-day moving average plotted alongside a 20-day moving average.

The normal interpretation is to sell when the short term moving average falls below the longer term moving average and to buy when it moves above. The buy and sell signals have been marked onto Figure 8-3 for clarification. The rationale behind this interpretation is that the short term moving average (in this case five days) represents a "current" market consensus. The longer term moving average (in this case 20 days), on the other hand, represents the market consensus for a period before the short term moving average. If the short term moving average is above the longer term moving average then "current" market expectations are for a higher share price. But if the longer term moving average is above the shorter term moving average then current market expectations are for a decreasing share price.

To show that this form of interpretation does, indeed, work I have taken Figure 8-3 and removed the moving averages but left on the buy and sell signals. Then I have plotted the underlying share price movements for Cadbury Schweppes shares to show that the signals did, indeed, work and would have produced a tidy profit.

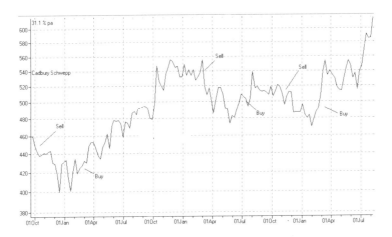

*Figure 8-4 The same buy and sell signals from Figure 8-3*
*superimposed on the real price data.*

Three or more moving averages may be combined on the same chart to produce a far more complex system. These charts, however, tend to be a lot more difficult to interpret and produce many false starts. If you are an aggressive investor you find that you are making trades all the time and that very few of them are paying off, whilst less aggressive investors find that they will make very few trades and the ones they do make will last for a shorter duration.

For both of these reasons I tend to leave them well alone.

# Smoothing Data

A side benefit of the moving average system is to smooth volatile data. If the value of a financial instrument tends to move wildly it can sometimes be difficult to see the underlying trends. So plotting a moving average curve instead of the basic price chart can sometimes give you a clearer view of what is going on.

Figure 8-5 shows the data for Tomkins shares and a 20-day moving average plotted on a separate chart. You can see that the lower chart is easier to interpret and removes a lot of the noise, which is apparent on the share price movement.

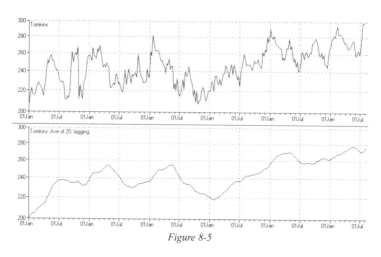

*Figure 8-5*

# Summary

- Moving averages are one of the oldest and most popular technical analysis tools -particularly amongst day traders.

- The moving average is the average price of a financial instrument at a given time.

- Moving averages can be calculated for any period to give you short, medium and long term views on the movement of a share price.

- A simple moving average is calculated by adding together the closing prices of a financial instrument over a certain number of time periods and then dividing the sum by the number of periods involved.

- Most day traders buy when a shares price rises above its moving average, and...

- Sell when the shares price falls below its moving average

## Chapter Nine

# Advanced Trading Strategies

## Part II

---

**Key Concept:**
Indicators and oscillators are two more technical analysis tools commonly used by day traders to help them open and close the right kind of trading positions at the right time.

---

In its simplest form, an indicator is an arithmetical calculation made on the basis of fluctuations in the price of a financial instrument and/or the volume associated with it. The resultant value is then used to predict future changes in prices. In other words it is giving an "indication" of what is to come.

An "oscillator" is very similar to an indicator in that it predicts future changes in the price movement of a financial instrument. However an oscillator should strictly be "normalised". This means that all values are changed so that they fall between +1 and -1, or alternatively +100% and -100%. This is achieved by taking the indicator and dividing all of the available data by the maximum possible value.

To see how this works, let's look at the momentum indicator.

# Momentum

The basic **momentum indicator** is one of the simplest technical analysis equations available. It is a calculation of the difference between the current market price of an instrument and the price of a same instrument a certain number of days ago.

**The momentum indicator =**
**(current value - value N days ago)**

The number of days, N, will depend on your interest in the market. If you are a regular trader then you will use a low value for N, but if you are building a pension portfolio then you will use a large value for N.

To use this momentum indicator in its raw form you would simply buy the financial instrument when the indicator becomes positive

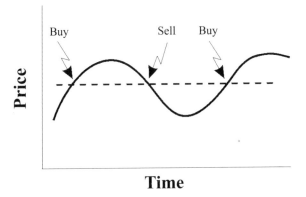

*Figure 9-1 Price momentum indicator*

and sell when it turns negative. In other words you are buying when the price is picking up momentum and selling when that momentum has been lost. Again, like many other analysis tools in this book, it is a lagging technique and you will enter the market after it has made a turn or reversal. But although you will miss the beginning of the change you should be able to participate in the main action.

To convert the momentum indicator into a true oscillator you now need to divide by the maximum obtainable momentum value. Some markets such as the commodity markets and the American T-Bill market set a limit on the maximum change allowed in one day. This gives you an obvious Figure with which to divide your momentum indicator. However most markets do not operate in this manner. Instead you need to set an arbitrary limit which will give you a general idea of price movement in your expected time frame.

Such a limit, for the ordinary investor, could be a period of one year. Look back over the price fluctuations for the last 12 months and calculate the momentum indicator throughout the year. Then run through the resultant data and find the maximum and minimum momentum indicator that you have calculated. Finally, to calculate your momentum oscillator, divide all the data you have calculated for the year by the larger of the maximum or minimum. You will now be able to plot your momentum oscillator and see that, although it has the same shape as the momentum indicator, the scales are easier to understand.

You now use this new chart to calculate when a market is "overbought" or "oversold". In an overbought market virtually all the investors who had intended buying a particular financial instrument have already committed the money that they are using to invest. Any further influx of money in favour of that instrument is possibly coming from short term speculators or less informed investors who are simply jumping on the band wagon. Naturally an oversold market is one in which the smart money has already switched out or gone short and any further price drop can also be attributed to the "me too" syndrome.

Exactly when the momentum oscillator indicates that the market for a financial instrument is overbought or oversold is almost as arbitrary as setting out the maximum and minimum indicator levels or the value for N in your original momentum calculation. Remember technical analysis, as we have said before, is as much an art as a science.

The answer lies in whether your aim is to lag or to lead the market.

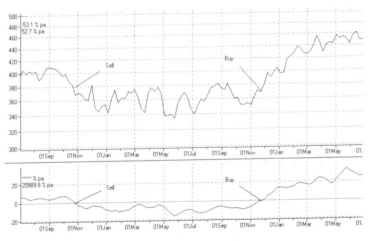

*Figure 9-2 Using the Momentum Indicator to buy and sell Opeco shares*

If you are quite happy to enter a market once a change has already taken place and simply profit from the majority of a price change then you will quite happy to use a momentum indicator (or any other indicator) to trade with the trend. In other words you will use the oscillator to buy and sell whenever it crosses the zero line and make your move according to its direction.

If your aim is to beat the market you will be intending to make your move before a new trend takes hold. In this situation you are looking to make your trades when the momentum oscillator is at a peak or a trough. Obviously you do not know when this is going to occur because the oscillator does not always reach right up to +1 or -1. So, instead, you should aim to make your trades when the oscillator reaches, say, 0.8 or above. With such a strategy you will be going against the short-term trend and essentially taking a punt on the chances of a technical reaction occurring.

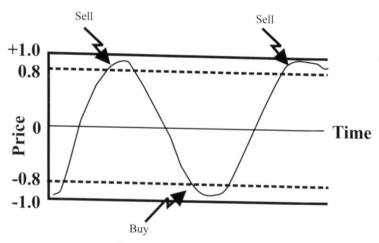

*Figure 9-3 Buying and selling ahead*
*of the market using the Momentum Oscillator*

# Rate of Change

The Rate of Change indicator (ROC) is a way of showing how rapidly the price of a particular financial instrument is moving. The underlying principle is that if a price is rising (or falling) very quickly there will soon come a time when it is thought to be overbought (or oversold). When this occurs the price may still continue to rise (or fall), but not as rapidly as it was before.

This oscillator always has a value between zero and 10 and is calculated from the average of all price rises in a given period divided by the average of all price falls in the same period.

Again the choice of period is arbitrary and dependent on your position in the markets.

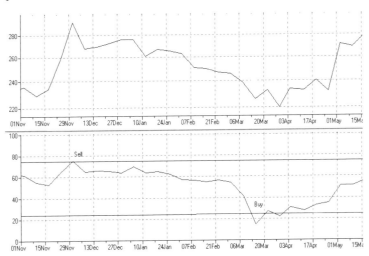

*Figure 9-4 Selling and then buying signals*
*from the Rate of Change oscillator*

The rate of change indicator is :

$$ROC = 100 - 100/(1+X)$$

where

**X = (average of price rises) / (average of price falls)**

The neutral position of this oscillator is at 50; if it rises above then the instrument is becoming overbought, if it falls below it is becoming oversold. Critical levels exist at 75 and 25. An ROC above or below these levels indicate the instrument is very overbought or very oversold, and a price reversal is considered extremely imminent.

# Price Minus Average

If you take a price chart and superimpose the moving average over top you will see the price is sometimes above the average and

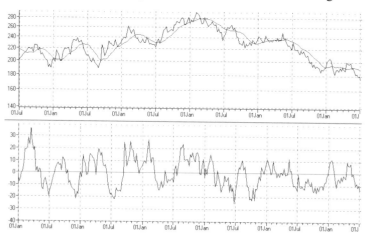

*Figure 8-5  Price Minus Average oscillator in operation*

at other times below. The Price Minus Average is simply the difference between the two curves. So when the price and moving average curves cross one another the Price Minus Average oscillator will be at the value zero, when the price is above the average it will be positive and when the price is below the average it will be negative.

This oscillator allows you to see clearly how big the difference is between the current price and a long-term average figure. To obtain buy and sell signals, follow the same routine as you did with the momentum indicator and divide your data by the larger of the maximum or minimum obtained over a certain period. You can then set your buy and sell signals when the curve crosses the zero line (lagging the market) or at a high percentage of the normalised value such as 0.8 or 0.9 (leading the market).

# Moving Average Convergence/ Divergence (MACD)

This is a simple modification of the average chart to show divergence (or convergence) of two separate moving averages. One of these moving averages will be calculated for the short term and one for a longer term.

When the instrument is trending in one direction, say upwards, the shorter term moving average will rise quicker than the longer term moving average.

The difference between these two averages is calculated and then normalised in the usual manner. As the MACD falls below or rises above the zero line it forecasts that the instrument will fall or rise corresponding as supply/demand lines move up and down in line with investor expectations. The further the MACD moves from the benchmark zero line, the stronger the trend is likely to be.

A variation used on the MACD by many analysts is known as the "signal line". This is used to help you lead the market and anticipate the convergence of the two moving averages. Plot your MACD in the usual way and then superimpose a moving average of the MACD itself (not of the underlying financial instrument price). You should then buy when the MACD moves above the signal line and sell when it moves below.

# The Relative Strength Index (RSI)

This oscillates between an upper limit of 100 and a lower limit of zero. If the RSI is above 70 then the market is thought to be over-bought and the forecast is for a fall. If the RSI is below 30 then the market is thought to be oversold and the forecast is for a rise.

You calculate the relative strength index by;

$$RSI = 100 - \left( \frac{100}{\Sigma \, (+ \text{ changes} \, / - \text{ changes}) + 1} \right)$$

# Volume Accumulation Indicator

This technical indicator was created by Marc Chaikin and it measures trading volume in relation to price fluctuations. It works on the hypothesis that if a market spends most of the day on a downward trend, but ends on a positive note, the positive trend should be interpreted in relation to the whole which was largely negative.

So, the Volume Accumulation Formula looks like this:

$$VA = [((MC-ML) - (MH-MC)) / (MH-ML)] \times V$$

where VA is volume accumulation, MC is the market close, ML is the market low, MH is the market high and V is the volume.

The volume accumulator line should now be compared to the basic price line and look for divergences between the two trends. For example, if the volume accumulator line fails to confirm an upward price trend (divergence of the two lines), a fall in the underlying instrument price is being indicated.

# Summary

◆ In its simplest form, an indicator is an arithmetical calculation made on the basis of fluctuations in the price of a financial instrument and/or the volume associated with it. The resultant value is then used to predict future changes in prices.

◆ An "oscillator" is very similar to an indicator in that it predicts future changes in the price movement of a financial instrument.

◆ The basic momentum indicator is one of the simplest technical analysis equations available. It is a calculation of the difference between the current market price of an instrument and the price of a same instrument a certain number of days ago.

◆ The Rate of Change indicator (ROC) is a way of showing how rapidly the price of a particular financial instrument is moving.

◆ The Relative Strength Indicator (RSI) oscillates between an upper limit of 100 and a lower limit of zero.

◆ If the RSI is above 70 then the market is thought to be overbought and the forecast is for a fall.

◆ If the RSI is below 30 then the market is thought to be oversold and the forecast is for a rise.

# Conclusion

Now that we have taken our whistle-stop tour around the world of day trading you should have enough information to decide for yourself whether becoming a day trader is something that you personally would be interested in. If the answer is yes then this is just the beginning for you. Your next step is to study the subject in more detail and teach yourself (or have someone else teach you) how to turn the principles of day trading into profit.

If the answer is no, then at least this concise guide has enable you to make that decision based on knowledge rather than pre-conceived ideas of what day trading is all about.

The only question which remains to be answered is this: Is day trading merely a passing craze, or is it truly something that is here to stay?

In my opinion, day trading is here to stay. As computer technology continues making great advances, as more and more individuals gain access to the internet and as we as a society place increasing value on personal and financial freedom, so I believe that day trading will become even bigger in terms of popularity.

The future of day trading, as I see it, is a promising one. There will come a day when day trading as an occupation is as common as any other. And that day won't be in twenty or thirty years time. I believe we are even now standing on the brink of a day trading revolution that will affect all of us in some way.

Here's to the future!